SOLOS FOR THE SANCTUARY
SEASONS
OVER 20 PIANO SOLOS FOR THE CHURCH YEAR

Arranged by Glenda Austin

ISBN 978-1-70515-820-3

Willis Music

EXCLUSIVELY DISTRIBUTED BY

HAL•LEONARD®

Visit Hal Leonard Online at
www.halleonard.com

World headquarters, contact:
Hal Leonard
7777 West Bluemound Road
Milwaukee, WI 53213
Email: info@halleonard.com

In Europe, contact:
Hal Leonard Europe Limited
1 Red Place
London, W1K 6PL
Email: info@halleonardeurope.com

In Australia, contact:
Hal Leonard Australia Pty. Ltd.
4 Lentara Court
Cheltenham, Victoria, 3192 Australia
Email: info@halleonard.com.au

ABOUT THE ARRANGER

Glenda Austin was born and raised in Joplin, Missouri. She has vast experience as a church musician, beginning with her early years in the Baptist church, where she performed solos and improvised duets with her older sister Gloria on the organ.

Recently retired from a lifetime of general music teaching, Glenda continues to be a pianist for various chamber and concert choirs at Missouri Southern State University. Along with composing and arranging, she regularly hosts Facebook Lives from her living room piano. She also has an active YouTube channel that showcases her diverse piano styles.

Glenda received her music degrees from the University of Missouri at Columbia. She is married to David, her hometown high school sweetheart, and they enjoy spending time with their family.

PREFACE

I am pleased to present the latest addition to the family of Solos for the Sanctuary! *Seasons* took a while to pull together. There were many great hymns from which to choose, and I wanted to include many of my favorites. I believe the collection includes many of YOUR favorites, too. You can play from it year-round as the liturgical year unfolds.

About the arrangements: it's very difficult to notate exactly how these should be played. I want you to play them as you feel. My directions are very general, so you'll need to put yourself in the music and play from your heart. Be creative! I very seldom play something the same way twice. Often, I have to read from my own music to play exactly what I notated! And if you want to add a *ritard*, please do! If you want to play louder, softer, slower, faster, please do! And if you find that some of the chords are a bit large for your hands (like me), please feel free to omit a note or roll them! I do that frequently. Every arrangement is new. Even though I've played each one hundreds of times for congregational singing, these are all fresh and original. You'll hear some unexpected and interesting chords and certainly some jazz sounds. I enjoy the challenge of re-harmonizing standard tunes. And thanks to technology, you can hear the entire Solos for the Sanctuary series on my YouTube channel (played by me)!

May God bless you as you use your talents to serve the Lord. "Each of you should use whatever gift you have received to serve others as faithful stewards of God's grace in its various forms." *1 Peter 4:10*

Glenda Austin

Suggestions for Performing
According to the Church Season/Month

(This can vary from denomination to denomination.)

CONTENTS

Meditation 1

Words and Music by
Glenda Austin

Meditation 2

Glenda Austin

Unhurried and relaxed

Advent Carol

Traditional French Carol
Arranged by Glenda Austin

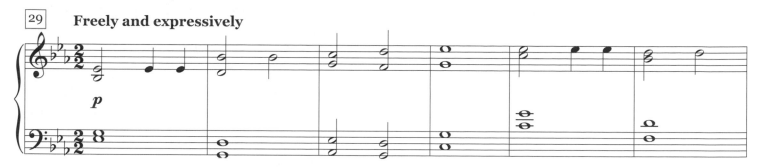

9

Freely and expressively

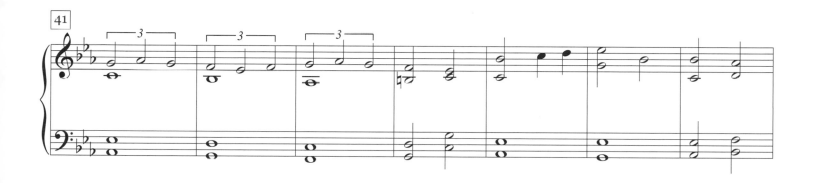

Tempo I

All Hail the Power of Jesus' Name

Words by Edward Perronet
Arranged by Glenda Austin

With majesty

CORONATION
Music by Oliver Holden

broadening

DIADEM
Music by James Ellor

In the Garden

Words and Music by C. Austin Miles
Arranged by Glenda Austin

Come, Ye Thankful People, Come

Words by Henry Alford
Music by George Job Elvey
Arranged by Glenda Austin

More movement

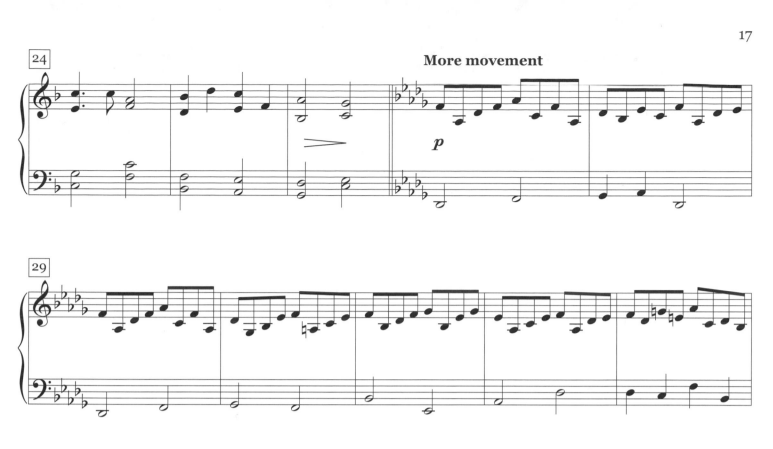

Jesus, Keep Me Near the Cross

Words by Fanny J. Crosby
Music by William H. Doane
Arranged by Glenda Austin

O Come, All Ye Faithful

Music by John Francis Wade
Arranged by Glenda Austin

Joyful and majestic

Pedal as needed

Let Us Break Bread Together

Traditional Spiritual
Arranged by Glenda Austin

A little more movement

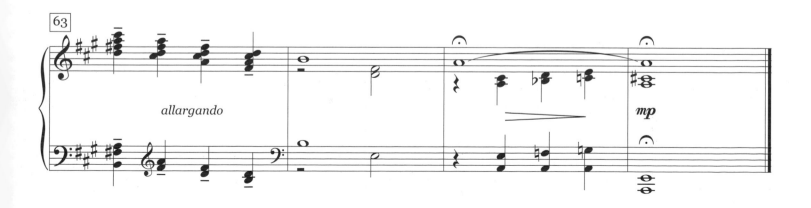

Living for Jesus

Words by Thomas O. Chisholm
Music by C. Harold Lowden
Arranged by Glenda Austin

With expression and flexibility

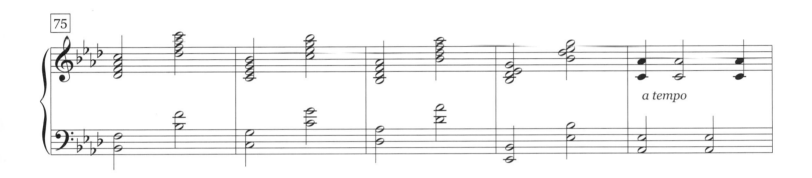

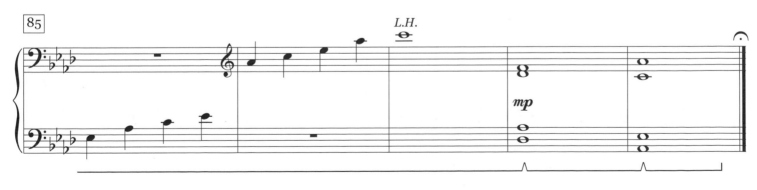

O Come, O Come, Emmanuel

15th Century French Melody
Arranged by Glenda Austin

Mysteriously

O Little Town of Bethlehem

Words by Phillips Brooks
Music by Lewis Redner
Arranged by Glenda Austin

* Quotes "Forest Green," an old English folk tune.

The Old Rugged Cross

Words and Music by Rev. George Bennard
Arranged by Glenda Austin

Unhurried

Open My Eyes, That I May See

Words and Music by Clara H. Scott
Arranged by Glenda Austin

Patriotic Medley

Arranged by Glenda Austin

MY COUNTRY, 'TIS OF THEE (AMERICA)
Words by Samuel Francis Smith
Music from *Thesaurus Musicus*

Freely, with expression

AMERICA THE BEAUTIFUL
Words by Katharine Lee Bates
Music by Samuel A. Ward

Spirit Medley

Arranged by Glenda Austin

Smoothly, not too fast

Pedal as needed

BREATHE ON ME, BREATH OF GOD
Words by Edwin Hatch
Music by Robert Jackson

HOLY SPIRIT, LIGHT DIVINE

Words by Andrew Reed
Music by Louis M. Gottschalk
Arranged by Edwin P. Parker

Sweet Hour of Prayer

Words by William W. Walford
Music by William B. Bradbury
Arranged by Glenda Austin

Reverently, with elegance and grace

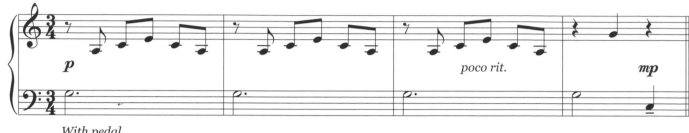

We Gather Together

Netherlands Folk Hymn
Music from *Nederlandtsch Gedenckclanck*
Harmonized by Eduard Kresmer
Arranged by Glenda Austin

With a lilt, not too fast

There's a Song in the Air

Words and Music by Oley Speaks
Arranged by Glenda Austin

This Is My Father's World

Words by Maltbie D. Babcock
Music by Franklin L. Sheppard
Arranged by Glenda Austin

Were You There When They Crucified My Lord?

Traditional
Arranged by Glenda Austin

Tenderly

Pedal as needed

When I Survey the Wondrous Cross

Words by Isaac Watts
Music arranged by Lowell Mason
Based on plainsong
Arranged by Glenda Austin

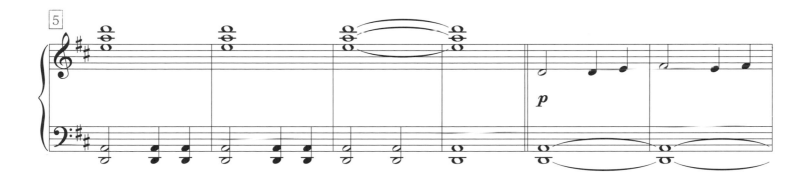

Doxology

Praise God from whom all blessings flow;
Praise Him, all creatures here below;
Praise Him above, ye heavenly host;
Praise Father, Son and Holy Ghost. Amen.

Words by Thomas Ken
Music by Louis Bourgeois
Arranged by Glenda Austin